Colin Teevan

Iph...

after Euripides'
Iphigeneia in Aulis

NICK HERN BOOKS
London
in association with
LYRIC THEATRE, BELFAST

Iph...

*was premiered at the Lyric Theatre, Belfast,
on Tuesday 2 March 1999, with the following cast,
in order of appearance:*

Old Man	DONNCHA CROWLEY
Agamemnon	SEAN HANNAWAY
Iphgeneia	MORNA REGAN
Chorus Leader	NIKI DOHERTY
Menelaus	RICHARD DORMER
Klytaimnestra	PAULA McFETRIDGE
Achilleus	KEVIN JAMES KELLY

Chorus   *on alternate nights*

JOANNE GILLESPIE	JOANNE GILLESPIE
BRONWYN HERRON	BRONWVN HERRON
RACHEL KELLY	ELIZABETH HUNTER
MICHELLE McCABE	JULIE McCANN
MARY ELLEN McCARTAN	ANDREA McPARTLAND
URSULA MURRAY	JANE MAIRS
SINEAD O'NEILL	KERRY MULVENNA
PHILIP HILDITCH	JOHN HODGE
BRYAN MARSHALL	MATTHEW FITZSIMON
SEAN O'RAWE	PADDY McKEOWN
PETER QUINN	PETER QUINN

Director	DAVID GRANT
Set & Costume Designer	GARY McCANN
Lighting Designer	PAUL O'NEILL
Deputy Stage Manager	SIMON FORBES
Movement	RICHARD KNIGHT
Music	DEBRA SALEM

Percussion arranged by Urban Strawberry Lunch

Colin Teevan

was born in Dublin. His plays include *The Big Sea* (1990, Galloglass Theatre Company, Tipperary), *Here Come Cowboys* (1992, Team Theatre Company, Dublin) *Buffalo Bill Has Gone to Alaska* (1993, Pigsback Theatre Company, Dublin) *Vinegar and Brown Paper* (1995, Abbey Theatre Company, Dublin) *The Crack and the Whip* (1997, Galloglass Theatre Company, Tipperary) as well as *Iph . . .* (1999, Lyric Theatre, Belfast). His latest work, *Svejk*, based on the novel *The Good Soldier Svejk* by Jaroslav Hasek, will receive its premiere at the Gate Theatre, London in April 1999. Colin is a founder member and former Artistic Director of Galloglass Theatre Company. In 1997 he was appointed Writer-in-Residence at Queen's University, Belfast, where he is now a lecturer and leading the new degree in Drama. Colin lives in Belfast with his wife and two children.

Euripides

was born in Salamis in 484 B.C., the day the Athenians defeated the Persians at that same place. He came from a family of standing but turned his back on the military and civic career expected of him, preferring a life of contemplation and writing for the stage. The most 'modern' and the most 'realist' of the great tragedians, Euripides was author of ninety-two plays. However, for most of his life he never achieved the popularity of Aeschylus and Sophocles, winning the main prize at the Festival of Dionysus only four or five times. Nevertheless, it is testimony to his enduring popularity that some seventeen of his plays survive – more than Aeschylus and Sophocles put together. Traditionally characterised as a misogynist, Euripides in fact created some of the greatest female roles – Medea, Hecuba, Andromache, Helen, Electra, Klytaimnestra, Aguae, Phaedra and, of course, two plays concerning Iphigeneia. At the age of 73 he went into exile at the court of Archelaus, King of Macedon, where he wrote his last two plays, *The Bacchae* and *Iphigeneia in Aulis*. When news of his death reached Athens, Sophocles, the nonogenerian playwright, appeared publicly in mourning for him.

Colin Teevan

This reinterpretation

by Colin Teevan of *Iphigeneia in Aulis* offers us a magnificently bleak version of a society in which a man is willing to sacrifice his daughter to appease a goddess and to further the political ambitions of his nation. Not for Teevan – and probably not for Euripides (since this is a notoriously interpolated text) – the cop-out of allowing a hind to stand in for Iphigeneia; she takes the rap herself.

I use the term 'cop out' and 'rap', terms which would not be out of place in the contemporary vernacular – 'bod', 'dreamboat', 'she just didn't give a toss' – on which Teevan draws to such ripping, rollicking, rumbustious effect. Striking, too, is his use of kennin-like compounds and neologisms, remarkable for their directness and depth of insight; 'Put off that trouble-face', 'I can't fullface you anymore', 'Look how even still she fatheryields to you'.

Most striking, most remarkable, is the uncluttered presentation of what might otherwise be a cluttered plot. Teevan's use of flashback is elaborate without being laboured, while the framing device of Agamemnon's fate at the hands of Klytaimnestra provides a context that is at once psychologically verifiable and dramatically viable.

The question of whether *Iphigeneia In Aulis* can ever be absolutely psychologically verifiable, given Iphigeneia's resistance, then resignation to the idea of 'I have no choice, so choose to die' may continue to concern those, including Artistotle, who might be troubled by such a volte-face. That said, Colin Teevan has given us a piece of theatre that is wonderfully robust, resolute and resonant.

Paul Muldoon, 1996

Leda and the Swan

A sudden blow: the great wings beating still
Above the staggering girl, her thighs caressed
By the dark webs, her nape caught in his bill,
He holds her helpless breast upon his breast.

How can those terrified vague fingers push
The feathered glory from her loosening thighs,
And how can body, laid in that white rush,
But feel the strange heart beating where it lies?

A shudder in the loins engenders there
The broken wall, the burning roof and tower
And Agamemnon dead.
                    Being so caught up,
So mastered by the brute blood of the air,
Did she put on his knowledge with his power
Before the indifferent beak could let her drop?

W.B. Yeats
(reprinted by permission)

Biographies

Donncha Crowley

Before taking up acting Donncha studied in Maynooth and in UCC and lived in various parts of Europe, Africa and Co Cork. By now he has worked with most of the main companies up and down the country. Recent roles were the Assessor in *Farawayan* by Donal O'Kelly and Mick in *Boss Grady's Boys* by Sebastian Barry (Arches, Glasgow). In 1997 he played The Bren O'Donoghue in Colin Teevan's *The Crack and the Whip*.

Other roles he likes to remember include Jimmy Jack in *Translations* (Bristol Old Vic), Dandy McCabe in *The Field* (Gaiety) and Jimmy in *Men* (Belfast Theatre Festival, 1992), Old Mahon in *Playboy of the Western World* and Pope Clement VI in *Red Noses*. Screen credits include *Angela's Ashes, The General, Stray Bullet 2, Father Ted Christmas Special, Pete's Meteor, All for Love* and *Miracle at Midnight*.

Sean Hannaway

Sean was educated at QUB and trained at the Central School of Speech and Drama. His first professional role was playing David in *The Rivals* at Nottingham Playhouse. Since then, work includes Drum Major in *Elgar's Rando* and Ferghal O'Connor in *The Hostage* at the RSC, Doctor in *Malfi* with Cheek by Jowl TC, Malvolio in *Twelfth Night* and Friar Lawrence in *Romeo and Juliet* with Imaginary Forces TC. More recently, work includes Antonio in *Twelfth Night* and Creon in *Oedipus* at the Northcott Theatre, Exeter.

Morna Regan

This is Morna's first show in the Lyric and she is delighted to be working here and back home in the North again. From Derry City, Morna studied at the University of London and Central School of Speech and Drama, and then trained for a further two years at USC LA, where she also worked professionally for two years after graduation.

Now resident in Dublin, work there includes *Emma* (Emma) directed by Conall Morrison, *Pentecost* (Ruth) directed by Lynne Parker for Rough Magic, *Sucking Dublin* (Amanda) written by Enda Walsh for Abbey Outreach, *A Tale of Two Cities* (Vengeance) directed by Alan Stanford at the Gate Theatre, *Poor Superman* (Violet) directed by Joe Devlin in the Project, and *Goya's Last Portrait* (Isobel) directed by John Crowley in studio for Field Day Theatre Company.

Favourite roles in Los Angeles include Maire in *Translations* and Minnie Powell in *Shadow* of a Gunman, both at the Celtic Arts Centre, and Faye in Joe Orton's Loot and Jocasta in Ted Hughes' Oedipus, both at the Bing Theatre, LA.

Morna has also appeared in a number of short films, most recently as Grainne in Elsewhere for Belfast company, Qubics, with Creative Alliance.

Niki Doherty

Niki graduated from the University of Ulster with a degree in Theatre Studies and English. After training as an English and Drama teacher, Niki has worked extensively as a drama facilitator both here in Northern Ireland and in the South of Ireland.

Niki's roles have included Susannah Walcott in Red Kettle's production of The Crucible and Rumpelstiltskin in Kabosh Theatre Company's NI T.I.E. tour. Niki recently appeared in Death of a Salesman and starred as Alice in Alice's Adventures In Wonderland, both at the Lyric.

Richard Dormer

Richard trained at the Royal Academy of Dramatic Art (RADA) and his theatre credits include Beautiful Thing, Duke of York Theatre, London; In the Heart of America, Bush Theatre, London; Una Pooka, Tricycle Theatre, London; Silverlands, Peacock Theatre, London; Three Sisters, Ipswich; Billy Budd in Billy Budd, Crucible Theatre, Sheffield; Too Late to Talk to Billy and All My Sons, Arts Theatre, Belfast; Observe the Sons of Ulster Marching Towards the Somme, Dundee Rep, Dundee; and the Lyric production of Philadelphia, Here I Come! which toured to both the Grand Opera House, Belfast, and the USA. Richard has just finished playing Harry in A Whistle in the Dark at the Lyric Theatre.

Richard's television credits include Casualty, BBC; Accentuate the Positive, Greenwich Films; Soldier Soldier, Central Television and The Young Indiana Jones Chronicles, Amblin Films. His film credits include A Further Gesture. Richard has also written two screenplays which are currently in pre-production.

Paula McFetridge

Paula was born in Belfast. Her theatre work includes Catchpenny Twist, Independent Voice, Can't Pay? Won't Pay!, and Gibralter Strait (Tinderbox Theatre Co.); Dancing at Lughnasa, A Midsummer Night's Dream, After Easter, Jane Eyre and The Taming of the Shrew (Lyric Theatre). She also appeared in The Patriot Game (Peacock Theatre); The Government Inspector (Dubbeljoint); Bondagers and Frontline Café (Charabanc Theatre Company) and To Hell with Faust (Big Telly Theatre Company). Most recently Paula played Mary-Anne in the Tinderbox/Field Day co-production Northern Star.

Television and film includes Crossmaheart (Lexington Films); Baby Doll (Fillum Ltd); 81 (81 Films) and Force of Duty (BBC).

Kevin James Kelly

Kevin began his career with the Belvoir Players and had spells with the Ulster Youth Theatre and the Belfast Youth and Community theatre group.

After successfully auditioning for the Royal Scottish Academy of Music and Drama he then moved to Glasgow, where he now lives.

After three years at drama school, Kevin has done various theatre, television and film work. From great acclaim for 'Joe' in Brian Friel's *Lovers*, to being nominated for a Scottish BAFTA for his role in a short film called *Smashing*, Kevin believes his richest reward has been able to work for director Ken Loach in *My Name Is Joe* and alongside Peter Mullen – the film's Best Actor award winner.

'I am delighted to get the chance to return to Belfast as an actor and make my family and friends who believed in me, very proud.'

Gary McCann
Set and Costume Designer

Gary trained at the Nottingham Trent University in Theatre Design. This is his fourth design for the Lyric, having previously designed *Tearing the Loom* by Gary Mitchell, *The Visit* for the Lyric Drama Studio and *Alice's Adventures in Wonderland*, the Lyric's Christmas production of 1998.

Other design work includes *Hansel and Gretel* at the Riverside, Coleraine for Kabosh

Productions, *The Tempest* at the Gardner Arts Centre, Brighton; *Capital Nights* for the Warehouse Theatre, Croydon; *The Swell* and *The Night Before Christmas* for Devon's Theatre Alibi and *The Quay Thing*, a season of ten site-specific performances on Exeter Quay.

Paul O'Neill

Paul hails from Dublin and has been lighting theatre productions for over 15 years. He designed the lighting for over twenty Rough Magic shows during the 1980's. Some of his designs have toured worldwide, notably; *Lament for Arthur Cleary* by David Bolger and *Bat the Father, Rabbit the Son* by Donal O'Kelly.

In 1995 Paul was assistant lighting designer on the original staging of *Riverdance – the Show* in Dublin and London. Recent credits include *Rosie and Star Wars* by Charlie O'Neill and *Farawayan* by Donal O'Kelly, both for Calypso Productions and Storyteller's production of Dickens' *Hard Times*.

Paul has designed for several music artists over the years, including Christy Moore, Paul Brady, The Rankin Family, James Brown, Nanci Griffith and Phil Coulter.

Currently most of Paul's work is in TV and the corporate sector, lighting conferences and product launches. He is delighted to be working with David Grant again almost ten years after *The Wake* (Fringe First award, Edinburgh, 1990).

Richard Knight

Laban trained dancer and choreographer, Richard Knight has been working in the dance world for six and a half years. He has danced with Transitions Dance Company, Divas Dance Company, Dance Theatre of Ireland and In Transit Dance Company. To date he has choreographed two dance pieces for theatre: *Pointer* in 1996 at the Bonnie Bird Theatre, London, and *Gate* in 1998 at Tower Street Theatre, Belfast, performed as part of Re-evolve in the Belfast Fringe Festival.

After completing a residency for the Arts Council of Northern Ireland and ArtsCare in Nov/Dec 1998, he has become more focused in his freelance work, teaching and choreographing in Belfast. At present he is working with theatre, school, community and mental health groups.

His future work will involve running his newly formed Contemporary Dance Company, Realm. He intends to continue his links with Belfast and will hope to tour with his company in Northern Ireland in the near future. He appreciates the opportunity to choreograph for *Iph . . .* and is thoroughly enjoying working with the team.

Debra Salem

Debra has written music for theatre, dance, television and radio. Her music for the Lyric Theatre includes *Playboy of the Western World, After the Fall, The Iceman Cometh, All My Sons* and *The Crucible* amongst others. She has worked with Replay Theatre Company on many occasions, including productions of *Mirad, A Boy from Bosnia, Permanent, Deadweight, Blood Lines* and other collaborations.

Debra has also worked with companies such as Big Telly Theatre Company on *Metamorphosis* and *To Hell with Faust*, Charabanc, Ulster Youth Theatre, 7:84, Leeds Playhouse and Theatre Ulster. She has been a musical director/composer for many projects where live vocals have played a large part, such as *Dockward, Snake Out*, the Lyric's production of *Around the Big Clock* and worked as Assistant Musical Director for Opera Northern Ireland's youth production of *West Side Story*.

In her capacity as children's choir director she has been involved with the last five summer productions at the Lyric – *Oliver!, Joseph, Annie, The Sound of Music* and *Little Shop of Horrors*. Debra is also a partner in Green Dolphin Recording Studios.

Simon Forbes

Simon is a recent addition to the Lyric stage management team, having joined during the summer production, *Little Shop of Horrors* after completing his training at the Royal Academy of Dramatic Art.

Shows before the Lyric include *Julius Caesar, Friends Like This* and various childrens shows with Stagecoach.

Introduction

'Where does it begin, then, this last tale of mine?
In day long gone, in Aulis
Where the sons of Danaos,
The daring Danaan Greeks, had gathered
To set sail for Asiatic Troy.' *Iph* . . .

'Where does it begin?' The recurring refrain through the
opening chapter of Roberto Calasso's masterly narration of the
evolution of Greek myth *The Marriage of Cadmus and
Harmony*. It began, he says, with the abduction of a woman –
Io, Europa, Helen, Ariadne, take your pick: the evolution of
Greek (and by extension European) consciousness and national
identity is mythologised in a series of tit for tat abductions
back and forth across the Mediterranean and Aegean Seas
between the gradually civilising Greece and 'barbaric' Asia.

But where did it begin? What was the original act?

Or, to put it another way, if myth is an attempt to explain
origins, then where did the myths themselves originate? That is
the size of question Calasso undertakes to examine. I will only
undertake, in this brief introduction, to explore how this story
of an adolescent girl sacrificed to the Gods for the furtherance
of national aims has come to be told, or retold, in the form it is
in this book, published to accompany its first stage production.
This, I suppose, is the tale of this tale and its tellers and
retellers.

By 406 B.C., the year of Euripides' death, his city-state,
Athens, and their allies had been at war with their fellow
Greek city-state, Sparta, and their allies, for twenty five years.
In contrast to the military glory of the early 5th Century B.C.,
when the Athenians and the Spartans had jointly repelled the
might of the Persians, this, the Peloponesian War, was a long
bloody war of attrition which had, by that stage, drained most

of the participants of their amassed wealth, their men and their honour. By 406 B.C. it was into its endgame. The Athenians were being ground into submission. It would spell the end not only of their political preeminence, but also of the extraordinary cultural eruption that was 5th-Century Athens.

Whether by choice or banished by his fellow citizens, Euripides himself spent the last few years of his life in exile at the court of Archelaus, king of the then semi-Barbarian Macedon. There is little doubt that, like the Old Man of *Iph . . .* , the poet had 'longlost care for man' and, more particularly, his fellow Athenian citizens whose vainglorious, vicious and incompetent conduct of the war had led the city to the brink of ruin.

And it was here, in Macedonia, that Euripides wrote his last two plays – *The Bacchae* and *Iphigeneia in Aulis*. Both of these plays were produced posthumously at Athens. *The Bacchae*, being the last produced, has usually been taken, along with Sophocles' *Oedipus at Colonus*, to be the final surviving act of the golden age of Greek Tragedy – 'the last tale' of an old storyteller. However, this was not the case.

In J. Diggle's 1994 Clarendon edition of *Euripidis Fabulae* – the most recent publication of the Greek text of *Iphigeneia in Aulis* – it is evident that little more than half of the play can be said to be *fortasse Euripidei* or 'probably Euripides'. The opening, the ending and many of the choruses are *vix* or even *non Euripidei*, either 'hardly' or simply 'not Euripides'. It would therefore seem likely that he died before he finished the play and that the play we know as *Iphigeneia in Aulis*, as Denys L. Page showed in his much earlier *Actors' Interpolations in Greek Tragedy* (1930), was added to, expanded, and concluded by, amongst others, Euripides' son (also called Euripides), by actors embellishing parts such as the grotesquely overwritten role of Achilleus (not a major role in the Euripidean fragments), and by comic writers of the 'new comedy' style of Menander (writing as late as 340 B.C). The resultant text is what the Greek scholar Kitto terms a 'thoroughly second rate play' (*Greek Tragedy* p.362). Of the now unbelievable ending where a messenger reports that just as Agamemnon was bringing his knife down on Iphigeneia she was transformed into a deer, while she herself is spirited off to

Tauris, Kitto argues that this destroys any possible catharsis. (*Greek Tragedy* p.315, p.365)

Even more damning are Aristotle's comments in Section 15 of the *Poetics*, where he holds Iphigeneia up as an example of inconsistent characterisation, saying that the Iphigeneia who pleads with her father not to kill her bears no resemblance to the Iphigeneia who demands 'Sacrifice me then smash Troy'. While I have omitted some of the more over-the-top interpolated jingoisms of the 'later' Iphigeneia manifestation, I do believe that her turn around in thinking is not inconsistent with the character of an adolescent girl who is under an enormous amount of moral duress to 'do the right thing'. And surely, in Ireland at least, we can understand the blind passion of the sentiments of her conversion to her community's cause. Finally, every character in the play changes their mind – Agamemnon, Menelaus, Achilleus – every one apart from Klytaimnestra. Surely this is part of the point Euripides is making.

I have always felt that in spite of the interpolations and damning reviews, *Iphigeneia in Aulis*, at its heart, is a powerful, if uneven, play.

Where did this interest of mine first begin?

I had first translated passages from the play at school in a Greek class which comprised two students and an octogenarian Jesuit who spoke and read over fifteen languages and used to thrill us with tales of the 13 declensions in Finnish. Even at that time, and in that sepulchral environment, Iphigeneia's major speech – 'If I could sing like Orpheus, / who touched the hearts of stones, / I'd sing so every rock and stone / would beg you not to kill me . . . ' – struck me as simple, evocative and moving. What I felt aged 16, I found out to be the case 12 years later – this was *fortasse Euripidei*.

And this was where I would begin in this process of reconstruction – with the *fortasse Euripidei*. I stripped away the additions and accretions and distortions, translated that which remained and laid them out to see if there was anything more than just 'the storyscraps of an agewrinkled fool.'

So, what is left with when one strips away the dross?

Certainly a series of unbearably tense and painful moments –
Agamemnon's dilemma, Klytaimnestra's fierce defence of her
child, Iphigeneia's initial refusal to sacrifice herself for Greece
and her ultimate acceptance – however, crucial to Greek
Tragedy, there is little quality material for the chorus, and
crucial to all theatre, there is little or no structure or resolution.

It was from this fragmentary material, a veritable scrapyard of
the most intense emotions that I started to see the way forward
– the literal setting of a scrapyard or post-industrial location in
the future, or some dystopic version of the present. It has
always seemed to me that in literary terms the Greeks repre-
sented their past – mythological, magical and larger than life –
in the same way as we represent our future in forms such as
Sci-fi and Cyberpunk. In both cases, past and future are simply
ways of looking at the present.

But to return to the 'storyscraps' in particular; there is a
nightmare quality to scenes which appear without introduction,
where present, past and future all commingle. This is the
remnants of a society – Athens of 406 B.C. – a society on the
brink of self-destruction, where factionalism and tribal in-
fighting has replaced any sense of *res publica*. A society
exhausted by tragedy, where political expedience has replaced
ethics and where the words of priests and prophets are no
longer fully to be trusted. Everyone has a personal agenda.

This setting also provided the key to the language. Greek
Tragedy presents great difficulties to the contemporary
translator; the biggest problem being that there is no such thing
as contemporary verse tragedy, and whatever occurrences there
might be of such a strange beast, there is certainly no widely
accepted idiom of contemporary verse drama. There have,
historically, been occurrences of verse drama in English, of
course, such as in the Jacobethan period, but the register of
such work is now itself as archaic as the Greek. If this retelling
was to be notionally set in some kind of industrial barbaric
present or future, a new idiom was needed: a tight, muscular
idiom like the original Greek, where perhaps a small pool of
five hundred wordstems stuck together in new and interesting

compounds would make us see accepted notions afresh. After all, Menelaus, Achilleus etc. were not 'kings' in our sense of the words, nor were they 'chieftains', nor 'lords' – terms which carry many extraneous cultural associations. In many cases compounds like 'fameglory' or 'faithfriend' which are used in *Iph* . . . are either direct translations of the Greek component words, or ways of expressing ideas for which English does not have singular satisfactory contemporary terms.

This muscular idiom also went some way towards regularising the rhythms of the piece. English, with its polyglotal Germanic and Romance origins, is very difficult to control tonally and percussively. I opted for as Anglo-Saxon a register as was feasible. It is the more down to earth, concrete side of English and has a far stronger, more regular bass line.

It is also for the sake of rhythm that I have shortened the spelling of Iphigeneia to Iphgeneia. While her father, mother, uncle and lover all have four syllable names which slot handily into most metres, Iphigeneia's comes in at an awkward five. Perhaps this is due to the origin of her name – discussed below – which is quite different to the origins of the other characters' names. French gets around the problems of scansion by translating her name as Iphigenie (pronounced If – i – gen – ee). I preferred the harder sounding If – gen – i – ah. The spellings of the other names, which might appear novel, are simply transliterations of the Greek.

The Euripidean fragments of the play *Iphigenia in Aulis* offered keys to many aspects of the retelling of this tale, but I still needed a structure.

Where to begin? Well, where did Euripides begin?

While the text of Euripides' *Iphigeneia in Aulis* has been adapted and added to by a variety of collaborators, and has also provided the source material for subsequent versions of the story by, amongst others, the French playwright Racine and the German opera composer Gluck, Euripides himself did not, as the phrase would have it, lick the story off a stone. The myth of Iphigeneia's sacrifice was one of the standard stories of Greek mythology; evidence of which can be found in Aristotle's *Poetics,* section 17, where it is used, along with the Oedipus myth, to demonstrate various aspects of plot development.

The mythical Iphigeneia's origins are in localised Greek cults based in, amongst other places, Aulis and Tauris – the two places Euripides chose to set his Iphigeneia plays. (Twenty years prior to writing *Iphigenia in Aulis*, Euripides wrote *Iphigeneia in Tauris*; the story of what happened her after she was replaced by a deer on the sacrificial altar and abducted by Artemis to be priestess of her shrine in Tauris.) Her name occurs as either Iphigeneia or Iphianassa, both meaning 'noble born'. Her parentage has been attributed in various myths to either Agamemnon and Klytaimnestra or Theseus and Helen. It would seem, however, that she is actually an early, pre-Hellenic, regional version of Artemis – virginal Goddess of hunting and the moon – who, with the spread of the powerful Hellenic culture, became absorbed into the cult of Artemis. Hence, the myths that evolved around her sacrifice to Artemis did so, perhaps, in order to explain her relationship to the Goddess. Like Artemis, she is always depicted as a virgin, and the bloodletting of her sacrifice, like the Goddess's association with the moon, would appear to be connected to menstruation and a young girl's growth to womanhood.

There are few and only passing references to Iphigeneia or Iphianassa in Homer, who predates Euripides by about 400 years. In Book 9 of *The Iliad* Agamemnon says that he will offer one of his three daughters 'Chrysothemis and Laodice and Iphianassa' to Achilleus in marriage in order to persuade him to fight Hector. This is the tenth year of the War at Troy. So, while this passage would appear to have the beginnings of the association of Achilleus with Iphigeneia, she has clearly not been sacrificed by her father.

The first major extant literary treatment of the story occurs in *The Oresteia*, Aeschylus' trilogy of plays – *Agamemnon, The Choephoroi and The Eumenides* – based on the aftermath of the Trojan War.

The Oresteia is the corner stone of Greek theatre. Written in 458 B.C. at the zenith of Athens' preeminence after their successful defence of Greek city-states from the might of

Barbarian Persia, it tells the story of Agamemnon's return from
the Trojan War, his murder by his wife Klytaimnestra, her then
murder by their son, Orestes, Orestes' descent into madness
and his ultimate absolution by Athene and the foundation of
the Athenian judicial system. It is a play written at a time of
confidence, wealth and empire building, telling the story of a
society's move from a barbaric eye-for-an-eye style of justice,
to one based on ethics and the need for social order.

While still basing it on traditional myth, Aeschylus makes
many innovations in his story of a family at war. One of the
most telling of these is Klytaimnestra's motivation for
murdering her husband. Traditionally Klytaimnestra was
depicted as the archetypal adultress who, while her husband is
away at war, conducts an affair with the pretender to the throne
of Mycenae, Aegisthus and, on Agamemnon's return, murders
him so that Aegisthus might become king. Aeschylus, however,
gives Klytaimnestra far more psychologically persuasive
motivation. The chorus of the old men of Argos tell how
Agamemnon was poised to set sail for Troy with the assembled
Greek forces when his fleet was stayed by a storm. The
prophet Kalchas, interpreting this as the will of Artemis,
decreed that he must sacrifice his daughter to Artemis;

Then the prophet spoke again,
Screamed against the winds
A new cure. 'Artemis demands . . .
Artemis demands . . . ' A bitter message,
Tears for the sons of Atreus;
They ripped their sceptres on the ground.
Then the elder Agamemnon spoke:
'Shall I disobey the god?
Can I disobey? the price
Is heavy. Heavy, too,
If I obey, if I kill my own daughter,
Joy of my life
If I stain my hands with virgin blood . . .
A father's hands . . . foul them with blood . . .
Before the gods.
And yet – how can I desert
The fleet, betray our allies?

They are angry, and they are right.
They want the wind to change;
They want the sacrifice,
The virgin blood.
So be it . . .
He killed his daughter. He killed her,
Bargained her death for a fair wind,
God speed to win a woman back . . .
Now out of sorrow may the good prevail
So prays Queen Klytaimnestra too,
The defence of Argos in her sole hands.

> (Aeschylus, *Oresteia: The Serpent Son*,
> from lines 195 – 257, Agamemnon,
> trans. F. Raphael and K. McLeish, Cambridge 1979.)

In these few lines – the full text of this single chorus runs to
210 lines – we can see not only Klytaimnestra's motivation for
murdering her husband, but also the crux of Agamemnon's
dilemma in Euripides' later treatment of the play; the debate
between the *koinos* and the *idios* – the community and the self.
Agamemnon is a public figure, a leader, he must choose to act
in the interests of the community. Klytaimnestra in Aeschylus'
reading, is a mother. Agamemnon has traded political position
for domestic peace. She will not forgive him.

While this is not the beginning of the myth of Iphigeneia, it
provided me with not only a possible beginning, but also a
possible ending for my retelling of Euripides' 'storyscraps'.
In *The Oresteia*, Aeschylus tells us that the cause of the
internecine conflict in Agamemnon's house is a result of his
sacrifice of his daughter both in the national and in his own
political interest. *The Oresteia* looks at the effects of this action
while letting the chorus simply tell us the cause. *Iphigeneia in
Aulis* examines the cause for this situation – how it all began –
and suggests the effects. While using the same story, both
playwrights were using it to dramatically different ends.
Aeschylus writing at the zenith of Athens' pomp, examines
how democracy and civilisation evolved out of barbarism and
superstition – the initial barbaric act is not explored; Euripides,
writing at the time of Athens' decline, seems to suggest that
that the barbaric past has never quite been escaped and is

always lurking under the surface, even if veiled with the language of political conviction and democracy.

To begin then near the beginning of Western Theatre; the beginning of *The Oresteia*. A watchman watching on the roof of the palace of Mycenae for the sign that Greece has triumphed over Troy. Ten years he has waited. What has he been doing all the time he has been waiting? How did he keep himself awake? And what did he do when the sign finally came? Did he have a life to return to? And how did he feel when Agamemnon, whose return he had watched for for so long and so unblinkingly, was murdered the night of his return? And, finally, why had he not gone with the other men to Troy?

The working through of these questions was to provide the structure. The watchman of *The Oresteia* was the Old Man of *Iphigeneia in Aulis*. He was not taken to Troy because he had sided with Klytaimnestra over Iphigeneia's sacrifice. Yet, because of his part in this affair, the very sight of him was a constant reminder to Klytaimnestra, so he was exiled to the roof to keep the watch. For ten years he watched and, to stop himself going entirely mad; he told himself stories – like the exiled Euripides, the last storytalker, the last of the great tragedians – and the story of Iphigeneia is to be his last. The prequel to the first story of Greek tragedy, the story of 'how we first dipped our hands in our own children's blood.'

The last structural/stylistic problem to be resolved was that of the chorus. The problems of realising a Greek chorus on the modern stage are manifold. Their often long, tangential retellings of mythical stories which assume a certain know-ledge of the subject on the audience's part frequently result in dull delays in the action. Whereas in ancient times the chorus was meant to act as a bridge between the audience and the protagonists, these days many choruses can be barriers. These problems were compounded with the *Iphigeneia in Aulis* since few of the choruses were written by Euripides nor were they particularly good.

It is here that I have taken the greatest liberties. It seemed to me that two things were necessary for the chorus. First of all, that without losing the formality of a Greek chorus, they be of xx Iph . . .

a contemporary sensibility – so as to act as a bridge between a modern audience and this archaic world. And secondly that they, more like the choruses of Sophocles, be set on a journey towards a deeper understanding themselves. The action causes the chorus to change their views from the 'young dreams of love and fameglory', the Aphroditic view, to a more mature Artemisian understanding of necessity.

To draw to a close where I began, I am thankful to Roberto Calasso's *Cadmus and Harmony* for his retelling of the story of Demeter and Persephone, which provided me with the material for the only wholly new chorus of the piece. I am also grateful to the following people for their help and encouragement in writing this play: Christopher Fitz-Simon, Dr. Judith Mossman, Jean Bleakney, Dr. Maureen Alden, David Grant, Stephen Wright and Tinderbox Theatre Company.

So that, broadly speaking, is where this piece of theatre had its beginnings; a new version of an unfinished version of a choral version of a half-heard/half-known version of a sacrificial myth – well, theatre is a collaborative artform! As to why, in Ireland, in 1999, begin such an undertaking at all – that you must judge for yourself.

Colin Teevan,
Belfast, 1999

Selected Further Reading

On *Iph* . . . and Recent Irish Versions of Greek Tragedies

Rick Jones 'Degradation, Defiance, Dachau, Dublin' in
(Dis)Placing Classical Greek Theatre, ed. S. Patsalidis and
E. Sakellaridou, Thessaloniki, Greece: University Studio
Press, 1999.

M. McDonald 'When Despair and History Rhyme' *New
Hibernia Review*, 1:2, 1997.

C. Teevan 'A Barbarian Activity' *Stages of Translation*, ed.
David Johnston, Absolute Press, Bath, 1996.

C. Teevan 'Northern Ireland: Our Troy?' *Modern Drama* Vol
XLI, No. 1, Spring, 1998.

On *Iphigeneia in Aulis*

D.S. Conacher *Euripidean Drama; Myth, Theme and Structure*,
O.U.P., Oxford, 1967.

N. Loraux *Tragic Ways of Killing Women*, trans. Anthony
Forster, Harvard University Press, Cambridge, Mass., 1987.

G.Murray *Euripides and his Age*, Williams and Norgate,
London, 1913.

D. L. Page *Actor's Interpolations in Greek Tragedy: Studied
with Reference to Euripides's 'Iphigeneia in Aulis'*,
Clarendon, Oxford, 1934.

S. Reinach 'Iphigenie', *Revue Etudes Greques*, XXVIII, 1915.

Wasserman 'Agamemnon in the Iphigeneia in Aulis', *Trans-
actions of the American Philological Association*, 1949.

T.B.L. Webster *The Tragedies of Euripides*, Methuen, London,
1967.

On Greek Society and Theatre in General

E.R. Dodds *The Greeks and the Irrational*, University of
California, Berkeley, 1951.

E. Hall *Inventing the Barbarian: Greek Self-Definition Through
Tragedy*, Clarendon, Oxford, 1989.

H.D.F. Kitto *Greek Tragedy: a literary study*, Methuen, London, 1967.

Nothing to do with Dionysios; Athenian Drama in its social context, ed.s J. Winkler and F.I. Zeitlin, Princeton, 1990.

E. Rohde *Psyche: the cult of souls and beliefs of immortality among the Greeks*, K.Paul, London, 1925.

O. Taplin *Greek Tragedy in Action*, Methuen, London, 1978.

IPH . . .

For Madeline

*This playscript went to press before the opening night
and may therefore differ slightly from the text as performed*

2

Dramatis Personae

OLD MAN
AGAMEMNON
MENELAUS
KLYTAIMNESTRA
IPHGENEIA
ACHILLEUS

THE CHORUS: adolescent girls from Halkis.

ACT ONE

It is night. The Old Man is on the roof of a derelict structure.
He cannot sleep. Eventually he gives up, sits up
and looks up at the stars.

OLD MAN

You Gods,
Cut me loose from this life of tears!
A man should pass his dying years in quiet rest,
Not banished to the roof to keep the watch;
Ten whole years, bag-eyed and sleepless,
I've lived here like a dog, distancepeering . . .
For what? For fire. For the victory flames
That were to tell us Troy is trashed and taken.
Now they have come.
Beenandgone this morning dawnlight.
But though it's come,
Though we have won,
Though peace is danced
Through ruined ghetto streets
And Agamemnon now sleeps safesound in his bed,
I cannot shut my eyes.
I have forgotten how.
War breeds inhuman habits in the most saneheaded man.
And my habit was to storytalk nightlong to the stars –
– my true faithfriends.
I've longlost care for man;
A crazyhead, warlusty beast –
So, I tell the stars the scraps of nightmare tales
Longforgot now by the world.
Though muddled, half-remembered in my wrinkled head,
They sometimes make good hearing.

He chuckles. It turns into an enormous yawn.

The stars, they like to laugh at hero deeds of men.

Pause.

No, they do not give a damn for us,
And peace has come, or so it's cried,
And there's no longer need to watch.
So, sleep. Sleep.

Tries to sleep but cannot.

O, you Gods,
Must I dig one more nightmare
From the ashes of the world?
Must, it seems, if ever am to rest.
Where does it begin, then, this last tale of mine?
In day long gone, in Aulis
Where the sons of Danaos,
The daring Danaan Greeks,
Had gathered to set sail for Asiatic Troy.

AGAMEMNON (*off*)

Old man! She comes for me!

OLD MAN

Yes, I was an old man, even then,
And Agamemnon called for me
As he is calling now –

AGAMEMNON (*off*)

Old man! Wake up.

*Light reveals Agamemnon transfixed by
the apparition of his daughter, Iphgeneia.
He holds a letter in his hand.*

AGAMEMNON

(*Terrified.*) Come quick, please, old man!

IPHGENEIA

This is such joy, Papa,
It's so long since I've seen you.

Pause.

It was so sweet of you to send for me.

Pause.

Father, put off that troubleface
And let me see your loving eyes.

Pause.

I'm here, forget your cares
And be with me awhile.

Pause.

Forget your cares.

Pause.

AGAMEMNON

O Gods, I've not the strength . . .

He looks away to call to the Old Man. She is gone.

Old man! Wake yourself and hurry here.

He looks back to where she stood/appeared. Pause.

Still the sea and still the sky
And silent the winds, still,
At Aulis.
Dawn's white light has not yet cracked dark night;
There is still time to turn . . .

Pause. Recovers his composure.

Leda, Thestiuschild, bore two daughters;
My Klytaimnestra, and Helen . . .
That same Helen, whom every ghettoman of Greece
Desired to make his wife.
So sharp and keen our jealousy,
Violence, dread death and enmity,
Each man swore upon the other.
Murderous we grew toward each other.
And Tyndaros, her father wondered
How, without provoking civil strife,
He might marry off his daughter.
Thus he decided:
Make every Danaan suitor to a man,
With solemn binding sacrifice, swear

To stand by whosoever won her hand
Should any man – Barbarian or Greek –
Try to lure her from her husband's bed,
And to raze that bastard's village, town or ghetto
To the earth. This we agreed.
So did Tyndaros entwine
Each man's fortune to the next,
Then bid his daughter to decide
Which Danaan warman she might have.
My brother, Menelaus. That they had never met!

But, for a while, all seemed to hold together.
Life went on. Our oaths slipped from mind. Until . . .
Until, that is, there sailed from Barbarian Troy
Paris, Priam's son, who with his fancy foreign dress
And superficial charm, seduced Helen
Then stole her, the fairest spoil of Greece, home,
Home to savage Troy.
Well, Menelaus, a man possessed,
Tore through all of Greece
To remind us of our solemn covenants,
Insisting we redress the wrong.
And so the Greeks have gathered at this bay
– Aulis –
armed with spear and stick and swords of shining steel
And strong prowed ships as swift and fell as sharks.
And, because I am my brother's brother, I suppose,
They have elected me to lead this lunge on Troy.
If truth be told I'd now forego this fameglory.
Old man!

> *The Old Man has already arrived quietly on stage.*
> *He appears younger than in the previous scene.*

OLD MAN

Forego fameglory?
Is to be Grandmaster
Not the dream of every Danaan,
Agamemnon Anax?

> *Agamemnon only realising now that the Old Man is there.*

AGAMEMNON

So you have woken from your dreams, I see.

OLD MAN

I do not dream.
Sleeplack stings my eyes like acid.
It's my years that make me slow.

AGAMEMNON

I am jealous of you,
I'm jealous of all honest johns
Who journey through this life
Unrecognised, unrenowned and . . .

OLD MAN

Unrewarded?

AGAMEMNON

Unknown.

OLD MAN

These words are hardly worthy of a warman.
You were born a son of Atreus,
Born to bear the burden of high office.

AGAMEMNON

Well now I would forego it.
This windless weather stays our boats
At anchor here in Aulis.
The gathered Greeks grow mutinous.
They itch for action. They'll brook no more delays.
While Kalchas, soothteller,
Interpreting our stalled momentum, has determined
That for us to sail to Troy
Iphgeneia, my girl, my child, my own daughter,
I must sacrifice to the stonehearted huntress,
Artemis.
When I first heard this, without delay,
I told my man Talthybius
To disband the Danaan force.
But Menelaus with fierce yet wily words
Persuaded me the only course
Was to proceed with this dread deed.

And so I wrote to Klytaimnestra
To send our daughter and her dowry,
Saying she was to marry Achilleus
The sea goddess Thetis-son.

OLD MAN

And would Achilleus, cheated of a bride,
Not wreak a fierce revenge?

AGAMEMNON

Fierce and dread. He would.

OLD MAN

Then you are dead, too?

AGAMEMNON

He knows none of this. Few do.
Kalchas, for now at least, keeps it to himself.
While Achilleus lends his name
But not his knowledge.

OLD MAN

Still and all, a dread design,
You promise your child she'll marry Achilleus,
While you really plan to kill her –
To satisfy the troops.

AGAMEMNON

Stop. Stop.
That is why I've written once again.
And that is why you must leave now with this letter.
I have changed my mind.
Menelaus, Helen, the troops and Troy itself
Can all be damned.
This letter countermands the last
And tells Klytaimnestra keep
Our daughter safesound at Mycenae.
You were bonded as a servant
To my wife and therefore me.
You alone I trust of this inconstant crew.
You alone are faithfriend to my family.
So forget your years and fly.

OLD MAN

I'll speed, as best my bones allow.

AGAMEMNON

Do better.
Drive yourself past limitation,
And go directly there.

OLD MAN

(*Piqued*) I am your dutiful domestic.

AGAMEMNON

Dawn's white light cracks night's black.
Hurry, I said, while there's still the time for turning back.

The Old Man leaves. Iphgeneia reappears.

IPHGENEIA

Papa –

Agamemnon is terrified. Blackout.

The Parodos

The Chorus enter. They are young excited girls.

CHORUS

Our fathers restrain us,
They're always trying to train us
To be their dutiful daughters.
But we have skipped our homes
Beside the barren foams
Of Arethusa's virgin waters.
We hiked our way
Around the bay,
From Halkis on the strait,
To catch a sight
Of the Danaan might
Which will Troy annihilate.

Troy they will sack
And bring Helen back

From Paris that Barbarian bum.
Revenge is the food
To put our heroes in the mood
And Greece will overcome.

As we neared our quest
We stopped for a rest
In the grove of Artemis' shrine.
A stone was stained red
With the blood of the dead –
The huntress's heavy fine.
A flicker of shame
In our hearts did inflame
At our dark desires;
To see the mighty warmen,
The brave and noble Danaans
And their ships,
   And their swords,
      And their spears,
         And their skills,
            And their skin,
               And their strength,
                  And their . . . And their . . . And their . .

Crescendo.

Troy they will sack
And bring Helen back,
From Paris that Barbarian bum.
Revenge is the food
To put our heroes in the mood.
And Greece will overcome.

*The young girls huddle together at the front of the stage
gaping at the Greek heroes.*

CHORUS MEMBER

Look!

CHORUS MEMBER

Where?

CHORUS MEMBER

Overthere –

CHORUS MEMBER

Ajax!

CHORUS MEMBER

Ajax who?

CHORUS MEMBER

Does it matter?

CHORUS MEMBER

Yes. There's two.

CHORUS MEMBER

Ajax son of Telamon and –

CHORUS MEMBER

Ajax son of Oileous.

CHORUS MEMBER

One a deadly demon freedom fighter –

CHORUS MEMBER

And one an awful womaniser.

CHORUS MEMBER

Which one's he?

CHORUS MEMBER

Can't you tell?

She looks. There's a catcall. They all laugh at her.

CHORUS

Deadly!

CHORUS MEMBER

Well who's that there, then?

CHORUS MEMBER

Where?

CHORUS MEMBER

Discussing his discus-ing.

CHORUS MEMBER

Diomedes, of course.

CHORUS MEMBER

Def –

CHORUS MEMBER

Tres def –

CHORUS MEMBER

He's dynamite –

CHORUS

A bang!

CHORUS MEMBER

I guess.

'Oooooh, look at her!'

CHORUS MEMBER

And that's Meriones.

CHORUS MEMBER

Son of Ares.

CHORUS MEMBER

God of war?

CHORUS MEMBER

God, the bod!

CHORUS MEMBER

He'd do for me. He's deadly.

CHORUS MEMBER (*pointing*)

And there's my Odysseus!

CHORUS MEMBER

Your Odysseus?

CHORUS MEMBER

He's odious –

CHORUS MEMBER

Dirtbag!

CHORUS MEMBER

Slimeball!

CHORUS MEMBER

Scum!

CHORUS MEMBER

No he's not!

CHORUS

Yes he is!

CHORUS MEMBER

No he's not!

CHORUS

Yes he is!

CHORUS MEMBER

Well I'm telling you he is!!!

One of them sees someone. Points.

CHORUS MEMBER

I don't believe it!

CHORUS MEMBER

It's him!

CHORUS MEMBER

My love. My heart's desire.

CHORUS MEMBER

It's a dream –

CHORUS MEMBER

A dream come true!

CHORUS MEMBER

I'm going to faint –

CHORUS

It's . . . it's. ..it's . . . it's Achilleus!

CHORUS MEMBER

Achilleus!

CHORUS MEMBER

Son of Thetis.

CHORUS MEMBER

Achilleus!

CHORUS MEMBER

Son of Zeus.

CHORUS MEMBER

Demigod Achilleus!

CHORUS MEMBER

Semiclad Achilleus.

CHORUS MEMBER

What a dreamboat!

Pause. All turn and look at the one.

CHORUS MEMBER

Fleetfoot Achilleus!

CHORUS MEMBER

Freedom fighting Achilleus –

CHORUS MEMBER

Formidable –

CHORUS MEMBER

Fabuloso –

CHORUS

It's fucking Achilleus!

Along the shore he races,
Like a god he clear outpaces
Beast and mortal alike.
He alone could destroy
Those Barbarians of Troy
And the killer blow for our freedom strike.

Our fathers restrain us,
They're always trying to train us
To be their dutiful daughters.
But we have skipped our homes,
Beside the barren foam
Of Arethusa's virgin waters.

Troy they will sack
And bring Helen back,
From Paris that Barbarian bum.
Revenge is the food
To put our heroes in the mood.
And Greece will overcome.

Lights out. Lights up. Chorus is present but dispersed.
Iphgeneia appears again to Agamemnon.

IPHGENEIA

This is such joy, Papa,
It's so long since I've seen you.

Pause.

It was so sweet of you to send for me.

Pause.

Father, please put off that troubleface
And let me see your loving eyes.

Pause.

I'm here, forget your cares
And be with me awhile.

AGAMEMNON

I am not an animal.
I have not a heart of stone.
A letter's sent.
I'll not throatcut any child of mine.
So leave me now in peace!

He goes inside his tent. She is gone. Menelaus enters,
hauling the Old Man in behind him. He shields himself
from the Old Man's pathetic blows while he trying
to read the letter Agamemnon was sending Klytaimnestra.

OLD MAN

. . . Menelaus, Menelaus, give it back –

MENELAUS

Draw back you wrinkled dog, or you're deadmeat.
You're too loyal to your spineless boss.

OLD MAN

That is to my favour, not my fault.

MENELAUS

If you dare carry through such damnblast duties,
I'll favour you with such a fist
You'll soon see the error of your wilful ways.

OLD MAN

It was not right of you to read the letter.

MENELAUS

It was not right for you to bear
Such words of treachery as these.

OLD MAN

Argue that with Agamemnon.
But let me deliver the letter.

MENELAUS

I'll not give it back.

OLD MAN

And I'll not give it up.

Old Man starts trying to wrestle the letter from Menelaus.

MENELAUS

I'll give your baldhead such a beating
You'll give it up or die.

OLD MAN

I am prepared to die. It is my duty.

MENELAUS

A wholesome homily, for a dog.

Commences beating Old Man.

OLD MAN

Agamemnon . . . Agamemnon Anax

Agamemnon enters. The beating stops.

AGAMEMNON

What is it now?

OLD MAN

I am wronged;
By force he takes your letter from me.
Your brother does not love you, Agamemnon.
He goes against what's right –

MENELAUS

My words are more weighty than this old fool's.

AGAMEMNON

Then tell me, Menelaus,
What wrong warrants such a uproar?

MENELAUS

Look me fullface and you will know.

AGAMEMNON

Would I, our father's son, fear to face you, Menelaus?

MENELAUS

Then why the letter? What of the words writ here?

AGAMEMNON

What words? I must read it if I am to know.
Give it to me, Menelaus.

MENELAUS

Give it to you? Not before I show all the Greeks
The doubleness you dare.

AGAMEMNON

So you broke the seal?

Pause.

By the Gods, you're a sickhearted man.
Where did you seize him?

MENELAUS

I was waiting, watching, on the road to Mycenae.

AGAMEMNON

Why must you mind my business?

MENELAUS

I sensed that I would need to.
And I am not your slave, brother.

AGAMEMNON

This world is in some state,
When a man's not master of his home.

MENELAUS

You are a sideways schemer, you've always been.

AGAMEMNON

I'm warning you,
I am Grandmaster still,
Head of all the warmen. That includes you.

MENELAUS

Then let me hold a mirror to that head of yours –
And don't you in lofty disdain turn from what is true –
While I, for my part, giveword to be fair.
You recall how hard you canvassed
To command the warmachine to Troy?
You needed no more fameglory
But lust for power knows no satisfaction.
So, you grasped at every rabble hand,
You kissed their mewling kids with tireless affectation,
Your door was open wide to every slave's demand.
You promised one and all the earth,
And, fair enough, you got the job.
But, then, Agamemnon, you aboutfaced.
No more did you seek out your supporters.
In fact, you hid behind locked doors.
Office should not alter any man.
You should stand by your friends.
You are where you are now because we put you there.
When I saw how you had changed, brother,
I saw you weren't the man I'd marked you for.

So it's no wonder then
That when the Greeks came here to Aulis,
Your command began to crumble.
The Gods stilled the western winds;
The warmen, restless, itching for a fight,
Began to voice their discontent.
Some demanded you disband the fleet.
How downjawed you appeared;

What point in all that politicking
If you could not lead our strong prowed ships on Troy?
You asked me, your brother, what to do,
How might you retrieve authority.
I told you what Kalchas had divined;
That you must make sacrifice to Artemis.
You were relieved.
And without any pressure or persuasion
You commanded Klytaimnestra
Send your eldest daughter,
Here to marry Achilleus.
The heavens heard these things.
Now, you have aboutfaced once again.

AGAMEMNON

With a clever word or two
You'll make your own doubleness seem right.
You always do.

CHORUS MEMBER

The bitterness of brothers,
When they come to blows –

CHORUS MEMBER

Is bitterness like no other –

CHORUS MEMBER

Each so well the other knows –

AGAMEMNON

You've had your say, now it's my turn.
You being my brother,
I'll be evenhanded in my words.
A Grandmaster should maintain
His coldblood and calmbearing,
Even when he stands accused.

Tell me, Menelaus, why you storm at me so strong?
Why the savage face?
Who has wronged you, really?
What is it you want, really?
Is it not a wife you want?
A faithful wife who'll do you right?

The one you had, you could not control
And I'm afraid, it's not for me
To find for you a fresh one.
I'm not to blame for your present situation.
Is your desire to get her back
So all consuming, her who did you such a wrong,
That you would reject all that is right?
Or is it simply that you envy my position?
Whatever motive it might be,
It's bound to be a selfish one.
Am I crazyhead if I decide,
After heartsore deliberation,
To withdraw my first decision?
Or is it you who is the madman
Who, being rid of her who was your ruin,
Now wants her back again?
Those former suitors of your wife,
Swore to Tyndaros' oath
Out of hope for Helen's love,
Not love for you, Menelaus.
The Gods view such misguided vows as void.
Surely. They must do.
I, for my part, will not throatcut my child.
It is not right. It will not be
That you would once more have your harlot wife,
While my own life be lived out in loss
Through lawless slaughter of the daughter I begot.
I've had my say.
You rage on long as you like.
But in my family's affairs, I'm telling you,
I will be just.

Hymn to Aphrodite

CHORUS

Aphrodite comes in the form of a fly
That bites in the night while we sleep.
Some she lets live in a love that is calm,

Some she sucks with passion deep.

Keep our beds, Aphrodite,
When we're wed, Aphrodite,
Free from the gadfly's bite.
Let our husbands' arms
Keep us free from harms
And grant us your good night.

Aphrodite bit the Spartan Queen
Helen with a prickling hunger.
For a savage love, she left her home,
Now we are rent asunder.

Keep our beds, Aphrodite,
When we're wed, Aphrodite,
Free from all temptation.
Let a happy home
Be our goal alone.
Save us from damnation.

CHORUS MEMBER
That Helen is a traitorous jilt –

CHORUS MEMBER
Look what she's brought to pass.

CHORUS MEMBER
She must have known what she was doing –

CHORUS MEMBER
She just didn't give a toss.

CHORUS MEMBER
But . . .

CHORUS
Yes?

CHORUS MEMBER
She acted out of love . . .

Pause.

A love so great it drove her

To leave her country and her home;
I feel sorry for her.

CHORUS

What?

CHORUS MEMBER

I mean . . . I mean to say . . .
Her eloping and all the shame
Was caused by Paris's seduction;
And so, I mean, is Paris not to blame?

Pause.

CHORUS MEMBER

She's been talking to the men.

CHORUS MEMBER

I've not!

CHORUS MEMBER

She's been listening to their tales.

CHORUS MEMBER

I've not! I've not!

CHORUS MEMBER

She thinks a man could be the reason
A girl goes off the rails.

CHORUS MEMBER

I've not! I don't!

CHORUS MEMBER

Don't you see –

CHORUS MEMBER

Paris, like all men, could not help himself –

CHORUS MEMBER

When it came to himself helping himself.

CHORUS MEMBER

Aphrodite brought him to her bed.

CHORUS MEMBER

He was simply, you know –

CHORUS MEMBER

Penis –

CHORUS MEMBER

Led!

CHORUS MEMBER

Shame –

CHORUS MEMBER

Shame on you –

CHORUS MEMBER

Don't you know that men –

CHORUS MEMBER

They're all the same, men –

CHORUS MEMBER

Only one thing on their minds –

CHORUS MEMBER

Turning any inch they might be given –

CHORUS MEMBER

Into miles and miles –

CHORUS MEMBER

Please stop it –

CHORUS MEMBER

But we women –

CHORUS MEMBER

We should know better.

CHORUS MEMBER

Aphrodite points the way –

CHORUS MEMBER

Keep your home and keep your man –

CHORUS MEMBER

Or be prepared to pay.

CHORUS MEMBER

And pay!

CHORUS

That Helen is a traitorous jilt,
Now look what she's brought to pass.
She's turned us all against ourselves,
She just didn't give –

> *Klytaimnestra and Iphgeneia have arrived. They stand
> surrounded by a sumptuous dowry.*

CHORUS MEMBER (*whispering*)

It's her.

CHORUS MEMBER (*whispering*)

Iphgeneia –

CHORUS MEMBER (*whispering*)

And her mother –

CHORUS MEMBER (*whispering*)

Klytaimnestra Anassa.

CHORUS MEMBER (*whispering, terrified*)

Do you think they saw?

CHORUS MEMBER (*whispering*)

Do you think they heard?

CHORUS MEMBER (*whispering*)

Listen to me, Girls, not one single word!

KLYTAIMNESTRA

Young girls of Halkis
Lead us to our quarters.

> *The Chorus fall silent.
> Slowly they form themselves into an orderly group.
> They move towards Klytaimnestra and Iphgeneia.*

CHORUS

The nature of man differs one to the next,
But right and wrong are always clear.
Let Aphrodite's mystery point us the way,
So we may live forever free from fear.

Keep my bed, Aphrodite,
When I'm wed, Aphrodite,

Free from the blood of guilt.
Marriage gives, Aphrodite,
A tree that lives, Aphrodite,
But passion is a flower that wilts.

Menelaus and Agamemnon have witnessed the arrival too.

MENELAUS
Look, Iphgeneia and your wife Klytaimnestra.
They have arrived –

AGAMEMNON
I see, as does every manjack in the camp . . .
Look how they rush out from their tents
To see what's going on –

MENELAUS
They'll wonder why they've come.

AGAMEMNON
And what am I supposed to tell them?
It's too late for turning back. Too late.

MENELAUS
A marriage. A marriage would appear
The likely reason for their coming.
But to whom? They will want answers.

AGAMEMNON
You Gods,
How cleartell this heartache?
How begin to break the binds
Of these threads in which I'm now entwined?
Some God plays with me and my plans,
His cunning far outwits my petty wiles.
The rabble live with lighter load,
Unencumbered, they can cry
When the fates fuck them around.
Not so us people of position,
We must appearances preserve.
We are the slaves of our supporters.
Trapped helpless in their gaze.
What can I do?
I am ashamed to show my grief,

Yet it is shameful not to shed a tear,
Such misfortunes now enmesh me.
You Gods, were things not bad enough
Without Klytaimnestra coming too?
With what words will I greet my wife?
With what face can I look at her?
A mother must tend to her daughter, I suppose,
On her daughter's wedding day.
Though this father grieves at how
He must give his child away.
My fatewrecked child.
My sadstarred, fatewrecked child
Who will now honeymoon with Hades.
O you Gods, on her knees she'll beg me;
Father, don't marry me to martyrdom –

MENELAUS

Brother let me hold your hand.

AGAMEMNON

Take it. You have won.
I have lost, lost everything.

MENELAUS

By Pelops and his son, our father, Atreus,
I swear I will speak straight to you,
Not to serve a purpose, not from the head,
But from the heart. Hearing you just now
Two tears tripped from my eyes,
Sympathy and sorrow.
This war of words cannot continue.
I did not wish to wrong you.
I regret it and am with you now.
And this I say to you,
You cannot throatcut your own child
So my concerns succeed.
Why should you mourn so I may smile?
Why should your daughter darkly die
So my child may look upon the light?
Why break my brother's heart
To win back her who's broken mine?
I'll find myself a new wife, if at all.

I was stupid and selfthinking till I saw,
What it is to kill one's child.
Disband the Danaans.
Wipe your wet eyes,
It is I who should now let tears fall.

AGAMEMNON

Menelaus, your mercygiving is not missed.
But we have journeyed past the point,
Where once we might have turned.
Fate now forces me to sacrifice my child.

MENELAUS

But who now forces such a fate on you? Not me –

AGAMEMNON

Them. The warmen, the ghettomen of Greece.

MENELAUS

Just send her hushhush back home
To the safety of Mycenae.

AGAMEMNON

However hushed the sending back,
Her arrival here's well known.
And her reason for being here
Won't be 'hushhushed' much longer.

MENELAUS

I will keep the Danaans calm.
They will never know.

AGAMEMNON

Kalchas. He owes me no favours nor bears me no love.
He'll broadcast it to the mob.

MENELAUS

We'll throatcut him before he speaks.

AGAMEMNON

But we told Odysseus of our plans.

MENELAUS

You command the warmachine, not he.
Just silence all contention.

AGAMEMNON

But he's a populist,
A panderer to the lowest denominator.
He'll pose as the soldiers' champion,
Playing on their superstitions,
He'll appeal to their basest bloody instincts –

MENELAUS

His ambition drives him hard.

AGAMEMNON

He will standfast with the ghettomen
And say I swore a sacrifice to Artemis
And now I doubleback.
With such appeals he'll lead the lynchmob
To crush the clan of Atreus.
If we fastfoot it to Mycenae, they would follow.
And sack the Cyclopean stronghold
And flatten home and family.

The procession moves towards the stage.
Menelaus seeing this moves slowly back and off the stage.

CHORUS

Aphrodite comes in the form of a fly
That bites in the night while we sleep.
Some she lets live in a love that is calm,
Some she sucks with passion deep.

Keep my bed, Aphrodite,
When I'm wed, Aphrodite,
Free from the gadfly's bite.
Let our husbands' arms
Keep us free from harms
And grant us your good night.

Klytaimnestra and Iphgeneia have arrived centre stage.
The Chorus disperse. Pause.

IPHGENEIA

I beg you not be angry, mother,
That I've run to my father first.
I just couldn't wait to kiss him.

KLYTAIMNESTRA

It is fitting, Iphgeneia,
My first-born always had more fatherlove
Than any of my others.

IPHGENEIA

This is such joy, Papa,
It's so long since I've seen you.

AGAMEMNON

Those are your father's feelings too.

IPHGENEIA

It was sweet of you to send for me.

AGAMEMNON

I'm not so sure I would say sweet.

IPHGENEIA

Father, you don't look pleased,
Though you tell me that you are.

AGAMEMNON

The man who must command has many cares.

IPHGENEIA

I'm here, Papa, forget your cares
And be with me awhile.

AGAMEMNON

My thoughts are with you alltimes, child.

IPHGENEIA

Then put off that troubleface
And let me see your loving eyes.

AGAMEMNON

Does my face not show my love for you?

IPHGENEIA

Yes . . . but tears tumble from your eyes –

AGAMEMNON

Our future parting will be long.

IPHGENEIA

Why? What is this Troy?

AGAMEMNON
The place where Paris lives.
O that he'd never looked on light of day.

IPHGENEIA
Then you are going far away and leaving me.

AGAMEMNON
Please stop. These words cause me to cry again.

IPHGENEIA
Then let us sillytalk, Papa,
If only you'll smile.

AGAMEMNON
O Gods. I have not the strength
To suffer this in silence.

IPHGENEIA
You'll soon come home to mother and to me.

AGAMEMNON
That is what I wish for.
But no longer have freechoice to wish.

IPHGENEIA
I wish Menelaus and his stupid problems,
I wish all wars and serious things,
Would simply go away.

AGAMEMNON
Problems do not go away.
They pass from one person to the next
Till they devour those nearest you.

IPHGENEIA
Papa?

AGAMEMNON
Nothing, child.

IPHGENEIA
You've been stuck here too long in stinking Aulis.

AGAMEMNON
And something still prevents our setting sail.

IPHGENEIA

I wish you'd bring me.

AGAMEMNON

You too must make a journey.

IPHGENEIA

I do? Where? Will I go with mother? Or alone?

AGAMEMNON

Alone . . . Alone, without any company.

IPHGENEIA

You're sending me to some strange place?

AGAMEMNON

Enough, Iphgeneia, enough.
It is not needful that you know
Our plans for you as yet.
You are too young to understand.

IPHGENEIA

Just hurry back from Troy to me,
When you've beaten all those Barbarians.

AGAMEMNON

First we must make sacrifice.

IPHGENEIA

And I will lead the dance
Around the sacred altar?
Can I Papa? Please?

AGAMEMNON

I envy you your child's heart. Now, go inside.
It is not right you're seen out here.
Just let me kiss your white hand.
Too soon we will be parted for too long.

Iphgeneia goes in. Long pause.

KLYTAIMNESTRA

Agamemnon Anax.

AGAMEMNON

Klytaimnestra Anassa.

Pause.

KLYTAIMNESTRA
I hear Achilleus is some catch.

AGAMEMNON
What?

KLYTAIMNESTRA
I hear Achilleus is some catch,
But I want more facts about his family.

AGAMEMNON
He's of Asopus's clan.

KLYTAIMNESTRA
Asopus?

AGAMEMNON
What?

KLYTAIMNESTRA
He's of Asopus's clan? . . . Come on.

AGAMEMNON
Asopus who begat Aigina began the line.

KLYTAIMNESTRA
And was it man or god or beast,
Who then begat with her?

AGAMEMNON
Is this really necessary?

KLYTAIMNESTRA
A mother must know details
Of her daughter's husband's line.
 . . . I'm waiting . . .
Mortal or immortal?

AGAMEMNON
Zeus.

KLYTAIMNESTRA
No less.

AGAMEMNON

Aigina begat Aiakos by Zeus.

KLYTAIMNESTRA

Good.

Pause.

What son of Aiakos then succeeded?

AGAMEMNON

Peleus.

KLYTAIMNESTRA

And then?

AGAMEMNON

Then Peleus married Thetis, the sea nymph, daughter of
Nereus.

KLYTAIMNESTRA

Curious. And Poseidon permitted this?

AGAMEMNON

Zeus approved it.

KLYTAIMNESTRA

Zeus again, no less.

AGAMEMNON

No less!

KLYTAIMNESTRA

And what kind of marriage had they?

AGAMEMNON

A marriage most magnificent
Conducted by the Centaur Cheiron
In the forests of Mount Pelion.

KLYTAIMNESTRA

Who was it then coached Achilleus?

AGAMEMNON

Cheiron. So he might learn
The ways of the immortals.
Such a man is your child to marry.

KLYTAIMNESTRA

No less.

AGAMEMNON

No more!

KLYTAIMNESTRA

What ghetto does he keep?

AGAMEMNON

You Gods! He has a patch in the Phthia.

KLYTAIMNESTRA

Phthia?

AGAMEMNON

Phthia.

KLYTAIMNESTRA

And to this 'Phthian patch' he'll send our child?

AGAMEMNON

I would think he might.

KLYTAIMNESTRA

Might? Do you have no care for your child's future?

AGAMEMNON

I can think of nothing else.

KLYTAIMNESTRA

When do they wed?

AGAMEMNON

When the good luck moon is full.

KLYTAIMNESTRA

So, you have sacrificed to Artemis,
For your daughter's happy future?

AGAMEMNON

I am about to. It is the very duty that delays us.

KLYTAIMNESTRA

You must do your Godduties, Agamemnon Anax.

AGAMEMNON

I will discharge all needful rites, Klytaimnestra Anassa –

KLYTAIMNESTRA

You – ?

AGAMEMNON

All marriage rites, that is.

KLYTAIMNESTRA

You'll make me unwelcome at my own daughter's wedding?

AGAMEMNON

When the eyes of all the ghettomen
Are fixed upon us, yes.

KLYTAIMNESTRA

Why make the marriage in this way?

AGAMEMNON

Return to Mycenae. Tend to your other children.

KLYTAIMNESTRA

Leave Iphgeneia? Who will tend the flame?

AGAMEMNON

I'll take care of wedding torches.

KLYTAIMNESTRA

This is not right. You have no care for custom.

AGAMEMNON

It's not custom for the Grandmaster's wife
To mess down with the men.

KLYTAIMNESTRA

It's custom for a mother,
To give away the girl she bore.

AGAMEMNON

It is neither right nor good that
Electra and your baby Orestes
Be left at home alone.

KLYTAIMNESTRA

They are well protected.
Iphgeneia has only me. It seems.

She goes inside. Lights out. Iphgeneia appears.

IPHGENEIA

Why, Papa? What is this Troy to me?

AGAMEMNON

I am not an animal.

IPHGENEIA

I wish Menelaus and his stupid problems,
I wish all wars and serious things,
Would simply go away.

AGAMEMNON

I have not a heart of stone.

IPHGENEIA

If I could sing like Orpheus,
Who touched the hearts of stones –

AGAMEMNON

Stop. Stop. Please, stop!
I am not an animal,
   . . . I . . . I . . .

Lights out.

ACT TWO

Chorus screams in excitement.

CHORUS MEMBER

I don't believe it –

CHORUS MEMBER

It's him –

CHORUS MEMBER

And he's coming this way –

CHORUS MEMBER

It's a dream –

CHORUS MEMBER

A dream come true –

CHORUS MEMBER

I'm going to faint –

CHORUS

It's . . . it's. . . it's . . . it's ACHILLEUS!

CHORUS MEMBER

Fleet-foot Achilleus!

CHORUS MEMBER

Freedom fighting Achilleus –

CHORUS MEMBER

Formidable –

CHORUS MEMBER

Fabuloso –

CHORUS

It's fucking ACHILLEUS.

Achilleus enters and is mobbed. Klytaimnestra emerges

from her tent. The chorus fall silent then quietly disperse.

KLYTAIMNESTRA
Achilleus, Goddess son, I thought it might be you.

ACHILLEUS
It is Achilleus, but who . . .
Excuse me, but what class of woman are you
That cuts such a finedrawn figure?

KLYTAIMNESTRA
I admire your manners, Sir, and must admit
That you'd have hardly met my class before.

ACHILLEUS
I have never met a lady
Who would brassneck a Danaan camp.
Who are you?

KLYTAIMNESTRA
Klytaimnestra, Ledachild,
The wife of Agamemnon.

ACHILLEUS
Klytaimnestra Anassa, this is indeed an honour,
But it's not right we're seen, like this.

KLYTAIMNESTRA
Fastfooting it already? Stay, Achilleus.
Should we not shake hands, at least?

ACHILLEUS
I beg your pardon, but I believe that
It's not right to mess with what's not mine.

KLYTAIMNESTRA
Of course it's right, since it's to my child
That you are promised, brave Thetis-son.

ACHILLEUS
What? I'm lost for words.
You must be crazyhead to –

KLYTAIMNESTRA
It is sweet to see the warman blush
To talk of things like this.

ACHILLEUS

Klytaimnestra Anassa, let me assure you,
I have never courted any of your clan,
Nor has ever Agamemnon
Talked such things to me.

KLYTAIMNESTRA

How can this be?

ACHILLEUS

We must find out.
We cannot both be right.

KLYTAIMNESTRA

I am the subject of some joke.
Now it is my turn to blush with shame.

ACHILLEUS

Someone plays with both of us, it seems.

KLYTAIMNESTRA (*leaving*)

Achilleus, I can't fullface you anymore,
Feeling false because someone plays false with me.

ACHILLEUS

And to you, Anassa, fare you well.
I'll go ask Agamemnon what he means by this.

Old Man sticks his head out of a tent.

OLD MAN

Achilleus, Aiakos kin, allow me talk to you.
And to you too, Ledachild.

ACHILLEUS

Who is this man who stays us – ?

OLD MAN

A slave, I'm not ashamed to say,
Fate permits me little pride.

ACHILLEUS

Whose slave?

OLD MAN

Klytaimnestra Anassa's, herself.

ACHILLEUS

I'll stay a moment more. So say now what you wished.

OLD MAN

You two are sure you are alone?

ACHILLEUS

Enough for you to speak. Come on.

OLD MAN

Might fate and my poor influence
Save her I hope to save.

ACHILLEUS

You won't if you keep wasting words. Out with it.

KLYTAIMNESTRA

Don't hesitate for fear of me.

OLD MAN

You know I've long been faithfriend
To both your family and to you?

KLYTAIMNESTRA

You've been a sworn servant many years.

OLD MAN

And only came to Agamemnon
As part of your due dowry?

KLYTAIMNESTRA

You came with me to Mycenae
And have served me ever since. Yes.

OLD MAN

And that I hold your happiness
Above that of your husband?

KLYTAIMNESTRA

I know that, so speak, old man.

OLD MAN

Agamemnon plans to kill your child.

KLYTAIMNESTRA

Never! You have grown simple in your baldyheaded years –

OLD MAN
He intends, with his own sword, to slit the girl's white throat.

KLYTAIMNESTRA
O Gods, is Agamemnon gone completely mad?

OLD MAN
Sound of mind. Except in family affairs, it seems.

KLYTAIMNESTRA
Does some demon drive him to this?

OLD MAN
Kalchas, soothteller determines it
To be the will of Artemis
So that the Danaans might set sail.

KLYTAIMNESTRA
Sick and more sick grows this joke of fate.
And my poor child, whose own father schemes to kill her – !

OLD MAN
All so Menelaus might retrieve his wayward wife from Troy.

KLYTAIMNESTRA
Must Iphgeneia foot the bill for my sister's sluttery?

OLD MAN
So it would seem. The huntress Artemis demands her blood,
If Kalchas is to be believed.

KLYTAIMNESTRA
And what intended Agamemnon
By the contrivance of this marriage?

OLD MAN
So you'd willingly send Iphgeneia here to Aulis.

KLYTAIMNESTRA
Child, I've sent you to your death!

OLD MAN
Agamemnon dares a dreadful deed.
It will be the ruination of us all.

KLYTAIMNESTRA
I can no longer staunch my tears.

OLD MAN
Seeing you so cheated of your girl,
Causes me to cry as well.

KLYTAIMNESTRA
How did you hear of this horrific plan?

OLD MAN
I was to take a second letter.

KLYTAIMNESTRA
Telling what?

OLD MAN
Telling you not to send your child.

KLYTAIMNESTRA
O you Gods, what happened it?

OLD MAN
Menelaus, fearing Agamemnon
Might see the light of reason
Intercepted it, and me.

KLYTAIMNESTRA
Do you hear this, Thetis-son?

ACHILLEUS
I am listening, nor do I weigh it lightly.

KLYTAIMNESTRA
They misled us with this marriage
While they schemed to slay my child.
What place is there for pride
When my girl's life hangs by a thread?
I beg you on my knees, Achilleus,
You are mortal, but born of a line of Gods,
Defend us, revenge us, Achilleus,
In the name of her who had hoped to call you love.
For you I garlanded my girl
For you I readied her for marriage,
Not knowing I deathdressed her.
Achilleus, your fameglory will be tarnished
Should you not help us in our need.
For though you might not ever marry her,

As her husband you've been named.
No place, no time for pride, Achilleus.
Defend us, Achilleus, revenge us.
Save my child from death.

Pause.

The Threnody of Demeter

CHORUS MEMBER (*sings*)

Away down all the dark days
I wander the world, alone,
For loss of my child

*Pause. Old Man and Achilleus are gone. Iphgeneia stands
with her mother peering, terrified, into the distance.*

IPHGENEIA

Mother, a crowd of men are coming towards us.

Pause.

I am shamefaced.
Such young dreams of love I had.

Pause.

Such young dreams –

She is gone.

CHORUS MEMBER

Away, away all down the days –

CHORUS

First a flash, then a fireball,
Engulfing her
As she bent to smell the sweet narcissus.
The soft earth of the fertile meadow cracked in two
And Zeusbrother, Hades, broke forth from his underworld.
And riding on his nightblack horse into the light
He plucked the sweetest flower of life
Back down to hell to be his bride.

'Away, away down all the dark days
I wander the world alone
For loss of my child'

The mother keened
As she scoured the earth
'Persephone! Persephone! Persephone'
She rasped her daughter's name
And with her icesharp breath
Froze the land in vengeance.
The world shivered,
But none dared tell her of her child's fate.
She sat by a spring and wept.

Away, away all down dark days
I wander the world alone
For loss of my child.

And the waters of the spring replied
'Mother, Demeter, blame not the land
For the loss of your child
It only did as it was bid.'
'But where is she, my Persephone?
Why will no one tell me where she's gone?'
'Because she is where all who live will be.
But dread to be. She lives in death'

'Away! Away! All down these dark days
I've wandered the world alone
For loss of my child

I want her back'
The mother cried to father Zeus
'I want her back.
She, the sweetest flower of life,
Was ripped from me untimely
And I want her back.'
The mother cried.
And Zeus,
Moved by her appeal said, 'Be content.
I will command my brother, Hades,
To return to you your child, on one condition;
That she has tasted nothing of death's food.'

'Away with all those dark days
That I wandered the world alone
For loss of my child

And now she's coming back to me.'
The mother elated, waited.
The daughter delighted, skipped
Through grey gardens of death
'Away, away I'm free'
'One moment, Persephone'
Said Hades and touched her arm
'As one last gesture of remembrance,
Share this little pomegranate with me'
Without thinking,
Or thinking this but one small thing
To be rid of him forever,
She ate six seeds, before fleeing back to the light –

Away, away down all the dark days
Since she'd last seen her mother –

'My girl, my child, O my daughter, O
What have you done?' Her mother sobbed.
'One seed for every month of every year
You will be doomed to live in hell
And I doomed to wander all the earth and howl
'Persephone! Persephone! Persephone'
On winter winds with icesharp breath
In vengeance freeze the earth.

Silence.

CHORUS MEMBER
Iphgeneia must face self-sacrifice for Greece –

CHORUS MEMBER
Unless rescued by the hand of Achilleus.

CHORUS MEMBER
Each way a sortof union.

CHORUS MEMBER
Each way a kind of fame.

CHORUS MEMBER
I'd die to be bloodbattlemaid
Of Greece's handsome hero men –

CHORUS MEMBER
Just think; as they are lunging into battle
They'd be lunging in for you!

They laugh. Relieved.

CHORUS MEMBER (*kneeling, as Iphgeneia*)
Take me, father, Agamemnon,
Slit my white neck for Greece.
Marry me to all my men.

CHORUS MEMBER (*standing over her as Agamemnon*)
My child, you know that we are Greeks?

CHORUS MEMBER (*as Iphgeneia*)
I do.

CHORUS MEMBER (*as Agamemnon*)
And that Greeks must live by their freewill?

CHORUS MEMBER (*as Iphgeneia*)
I do.

CHORUS MEMBER (*as Agamemnon*)
And that our bloodbattlemaid must
Like a soldier choose her fate,
We are not Barbarians
Forcing victims to the knife?

CHORUS MEMBER (*as Iphgeneia*)
Yes, Papa.

CHORUS MEMBER (*as Agamemnon*)
My child, do you choose this quite freely?

CHORUS MEMBER (*as Iphgeneia*)
I do, Papa, yes, yes I do.
So paint your faces with my blood,
My fierce warlusty men.
And as you risk your necks for Greece,
Remember, mine was risked for you.

They enact the throatcut. Long pause.

CHORUS MEMBER

I'd die for Greece –

CHORUS MEMBER

Me too –

CHORUS MEMBER

I'd die for Greece and more.

CHORUS MEMBER

More? What more?

CHORUS MEMBER

It's the utter –

CHORUS MEMBER

The absolute –

CHORUS MEMBER

The ultimate –

CHORUS MEMBER

It's so completely very deadly!

Pause. The mood is broken.

CHORUS MEMBER

Iphgeneia he will surely save –

CHORUS MEMBER

He is bright and bold and brave.

CHORUS MEMBER

And she was not raised a calf for slaughter.

CHORUS MEMBER

She is Agamemnon's daughter.

Silence.

CHORUS MEMBER

Away, away down all the dark days
I wander the earth alone . . .

Klytaimnestra, Agamemnon and Iphgeneia who cries quietly.
An argument has been raging.

KLYTAIMNESTRA

Away! Away from us, you . . . you –

IPHGENEIA

I beg you not be angry, Mother . . .
Papa . . . such joy . . . I felt to see you –

AGAMEMNON

O my child, why do you cry
And look at me with such unlove?
Your eyes turn towards the earth,
You tumble tears into your dress.

IPHGENEIA

Papa, please, put off that troubleface
And let me see your loving eyes.

KLYTAIMNESTRA

Look how even still she fatheryields to you,
I must speak for both of us it seems.

Pause.

AGAMEMNON

What are you two up to now?
What new twist have you planned for me?
It's clear you two conspire . . .

KLYTAIMNESTRA

Agamemnon, answer me straight
When I ask this one thing of you.

IPHGENEIA

Let me see your loving eyes.

Silence.

KLYTAIMNESTRA

Agamemnon!

Silence.

KLYTAIMNESTRA

Tell me the truth!

AGAMEMNON

. . . If your request were reasonheaded

Reason you would hear.

KLYTAIMNESTRA

I will ask just this one thing of you,
And you will answer straight.

AGAMEMNON

What a Godaccursed fate is mine.

KLYTAIMNESTRA

And mine, and hers.
One fate awaits us three.

IPHGENEIA

Let us sillytalk, Papa,
If only you will smile.

AGAMEMNON

Whom have I wronged to warrant this?

KLYTAIMNESTRA

You have the gall to ask us that?
This is your reasonhead response?

AGAMEMNON

You know. Someone has told you.
Now will we all be blast to nothing.

KLYTAIMNESTRA

Well now I know for certain.
You have no further need to speak,
This silence is enough confession.

IPHGENEIA

I wish Menelaus and his stupid problems
I wish all wars and serious things –

AGAMEMNON

I can say no more.

IPHGENEIA

– would simply go away.

KLYTAIMNESTRA

Listen to me, I'll have my say.
– I'll speak in simple words

So you might understand –
The first offence I charge you with
Is that by force from Tantalus,
My former love, you stole me.
You throatcut him and grabbed my child,
Newborn, from my breast.
You then beat that firstborn child to death.
And when my brothers, Pollux and Castor
Twinborn sons of Zeus, made war on you,
You fastfooted to my father Tyndaros,
To plead for his protection.
So you slimed back between my sheets.
I did my duty to your home
And I worked, as you must admit,
To make our house a happy one.
Your palace prospered thanks to me.
The hunter rarely bags so skilled a catch.
I bore you three children,
Two daughters and a son.
But, not content, you now intend
To rob me of another child.
And if someone asks you why you kill her,
What will you reply?
So Helen might return to Menelaus?!
It is rich indeed to pay for whores
With your own children's blood.

What will my heart then whisper
When I return home to Mycenae?
When I see my daughter's empty chair?
When I see my daughter's dresses
Hanging lifegone in her room?
When I sit alone and sob;
O my dead child, throatcut
By him who first did give you life,
Struck down by his and no other's hand.
What will my heart then whisper?

I swear you will receive repayment
When you return home again to me.
Dare seat yourself at my table

And I will dish you such desserts
As you have never dreamed.
Do not, by the Gods, do not make me do
Such deeds as will damn us all forever.

And what will you beg the Gods for
As you push home the knife?
A fitting welcome home
For such a foul farewell?
For, surely, it will be so,
The Gods, they are no fools,
They do remember child killers.

And what of your other children?
Will you expect to hold them
When you return home from the war?
They would fear to look at you,
Let alone embrace you;
Who knows who would be throatcut next.
Have you thought of this?
Or is political position
Your only real concern?
Why not tell the Greeks,
If they want fair winds for Troy,
Then they should choose by lot
A childkill for great Artemis.
That is right. That is reasonheaded,
But you offer your own daughter,
While Helen who has betrayed us all
Sails safely home to Sparta?
I'm not wrongthinking in these things.
Be saneheaded. Save your child, and family.

CHORUS MEMBER

A father cannot kill his daughter –

CHORUS MEMBER

She was not raised a calf for slaughter –

CHORUS

Agamemnon, Agamemnon Anax save her!
If you can, at all, you should.

Pause.

IPHGENEIA

If I could sing like Orpheus,
Who touched the hearts of stones,
I'd sing so every rock and stone
Would beg you not to kill me.
I would sing, but can't.
I have only tears
And these white arms
Which reaching out to you,
An olive branch, implore you
Not to kill me.
I am young, too young
And light is sweet to look upon,
In death I would be blind.
I was the first to call you father,
And the first you called your child.
I gave you your due fatherlove
And you returned a father's love to me.
Will I one day see you,
You once said,
The wife of some great warman
Happy with your husband and your home?
And I replied, Papa,
That one day I would welcome you
Into my husband's house,
And return to you the labours
Of my bringing up.
I remember all these words
Which you have now forgotten.
For you now want to kill me.
In the name of Pelops
And your father Atreus,
Do not make my mother
Who bore the pain of birth,
Bear this double pain of death.

O, what is this Troy to me?
Who this Paris?
What did I do to him?

Or Helen? How can my death help?

Look at me, father, fullface,
So that when I'm dead
You will remember me.

CHORUS

That Helen,
Look what she's brought to pass –

CHORUS MEMBER

Such young dreams of love –

CHORUS MEMBER

Death –

CHORUS MEMBER

And fameglory –

CHORUS MEMBER

Had we all.

CHORUS MEMBER

A father cannot kill his daughter –

CHORUS MEMBER

A child's not reared a calf for slaughter –

CHORUS MEMBER

In the name of any cause.

CHORUS

O, Agamemnon, Agamemnon, Agamemnon Anax save her,
If you can, at all, do save her
If, if, IF –

AGAMEMNON

Stop!
I am not an animal.
I have not a heart of stone.
I dearly love my children,
I would be crazyhead if I did not.
This thing, this sacrifice I dare to do
Is dread beyond belief.
But not to would be doom
Absolute. And so I must.

Look at this vast machine of war.
Look at these bronze clad fighting men.
They cannot budge, we cannot sail
To raze the towers of Troy,
If I don't sacrifice you.
So Kalchas has decreed.
Please understand.
Aphrodite weaves a warlust
Amongst the Danaan men.
Our marriage beds have been defiled,
These bastard Barbarians must be defeated
Once and for all.
Should I ignore the Gods' decree
They'll kill me, your mother
Klytaimnestra, our whole clan.
It's not my brother who enslaves me,
But Greece, whose freedom I must fight for.
Greece must overcome.
Both you and I must give our all
For the freedom of our homeland.

*Lights go down. Lights rise suddenly. Iphgeneia and
Klytaimnestra. Iphgeneia clutches at Klytaimnestra.*

IPHGENEIA
O mother, a crowd of men are coming towards us.

KLYTAIMNESTRA
The frontmost is Achilleus, goddess son,
The man you were to marry.

IPHGENEIA
Let me leave, let me hide my face.

KLYTAIMNESTRA
You tremble, child.

IPHGENEIA
I am shamefaced.

KLYTAIMNESTRA
But why?

IPHGENEIA

Because . . . such dreams I had –

KLYTAIMNESTRA

Grow up, girl, there's not the time.
Our last hope now rests with him.

Achilleus enters.

ACHILLEUS

Klytaimnestra, Leda child.

KLYTAIMNESTRA

What news have you?

ACHILLEUS

The ghettomen raise a bloodcry.

KLYTAIMNESTRA

Why?

ACHILLEUS

Your child.

KLYTAIMNESTRA

The bird of omen circles.

ACHILLEUS

They bay for blood of sacrifice.

KLYTAIMNESTRA

Did anyone defend us?

ACHILLEUS

They roared me down when I did try.

KLYTAIMNESTRA

While you tried to save my child?

ACHILLEUS

While I tried.

KLYTAIMNESTRA

They defied you, Goddess son?
Who would dare?

ACHILLEUS

Every Danaan to a man.

KLYTAIMNESTRA
And your own men? The Myrmidons?

ACHILLEUS
They were my chief abusers.

KLYTAIMNESTRA
We have lost all, my child.

ACHILLEUS
They sneered at me,
Saying I was lovelost to the girl.

KLYTAIMNESTRA
What did you reply?

ACHILLEUS
I said they should not seek
To slay my wife to be.

KLYTAIMNESTRA
One man at least remembers
What is right and what is not.

ACHILLEUS
Her father said that she was mine,
When he sent for her from home.
One of us, at least, should honour that.

KLYTAIMNESTRA
What did they say to that?

ACHILLEUS
My voice could not be heard above the clamour.

KLYTAIMNESTRA
The minds of mobs are animal.

ACHILLEUS
I still intend to save her.

KLYTAIMNESTRA
One man against the many?

ACHILLEUS
My servants bring my sword.

KLYTAIMNESTRA

You have honour still.

ACHILLEUS

I only do my duty.

KLYTAIMNESTRA

You will stop the sacrifice?

ACHILLEUS

I will try.

KLYTAIMNESTRA

And who will come to take her?

ACHILLEUS

The lynchmob, led by Odysseus.

KLYTAIMNESTRA

He yields to the people's pressure?

ACHILLEUS

He gladly chose to do this deed.

KLYTAIMNESTRA

Some choice to be child killer.

ACHILLEUS

I will stop him.

KLYTAIMNESTRA

And when he takes her
Will he tie her up?

ACHILLEUS

Like a calfling, if he can.

KLYTAIMNESTRA

What can I do?

ACHILLEUS

Hold her tight.

KLYTAIMNESTRA

Will that save her from the butcher's knife?

ACHILLEUS

Our last line of defence –

IPHGENEIA

Mother, Sir,
Please listen to my words.
In vain you strive to save me.
It is a fearful thing indeed
To face the unfaceable.
But we must.
It is right, Mother, that you praise this man,
But you know we cannot hope to win.
So realise his fameglory
Will be damaged in defending us.

Listen to these words I have to say –
As I've been standing here I've thought,
Thought of that which is being asked of me –
And have decided I must die.
Die for Greece. Die for her hero men.
Die famously and freely.
Die by my own consent
With no shallow thoughts of self.
See now how well I speak?
To me all Greece now looks in hope,
To me it lies to launch
Our shining ships on Troy.
To me it now falls to fend off
Barbarians from our land.
And by my blood
I'll help to pay back
Paris for his rape.
I must serve Greece
And so win my own fameglory.
It is not right for one like me
To love this life too much.
Our lives should not be lived
For just ourselves alone.
I was born for Greece not for myself.
Myriad men stand ready armed
Myriad more sit at their oars.
Greece has been sore wronged
And these Greeks would gladly die
For their beloved homeland.

How can I cry out, 'No,
I do not want to die?'
It is not right.
Nor is it right that Achilleus
Might lose his life for mine –
A warman's life is of more use
For our homeland's cause.
And furthermore, how can mortals
Reject what great Artemis demands?
I have no choice, so choose to die.
Sacrifice me, then smash Troy.
Smash Troy and all those stinking Trojans.
That will be memorial enough.
Women will sing my glory evermore.
It is right we rule Barbarians,
For we are free and they are not.

Long pause.

CHORUS MEMBER
O, she is of a well-born mind.

CHORUS MEMBER
She seeks to serve the common good.

CHORUS MEMBER
I cannot bear to listen –

CHORUS MEMBER
I cannot bear to look –

CHORUS MEMBER
You must. We must. One and all.

ACHILLEUS
Though I wish it with my heart,
My head has not the words
To counter you.
But I will set my sword
Beside the sacrificial stone,
Should your will, through fear, weaken
And you cry out for my help
Seeing the dagger at your throat.

IPHGENEIA

Mother, why do your eyes moisten
With a swell of silent tears?

KLYTAIMNESTRA

I have good cause;
Heartache now is killing me.

IPHGENEIA

You have no cause to cry.
I am saved. I am and will be saved.

KLYTAIMNESTRA

How? What do you mean, child?
A mother always mourns
The dying of her child.

IPHGENEIA

You need dig no grave for me.

KLYTAIMNESTRA

You must have memorial. A resting place.

IPHGENEIA

My resting place will be
The sacred shrine of Artemis.

Silence.

KLYTAIMNESTRA

You have decided.

IPHGENEIA

Yes. It is my good fortune
To give my life for Greece.

Silence.

KLYTAIMNESTRA

Do you have any word
For your sister Electra?

IPHGENEIA

Tell her good-bye and take care
Of little Orestes.

KLYTAIMNESTRA

O, what will my heart whisper
When I return home to Mycenae?
When I see your empty chair?
When I see your dresses
Hanging lifegone in your room?

Silence.

How might I keep your memory?

IPHGENEIA

Do not hate my father,
He still is your husband.

KLYTAIMNESTRA

His conscience now will run him
A sore and fatewrecked race.

IPHGENEIA

He does not desire my death.
He does it so the Danaans might be free.

KLYTAIMNESTRA

He did it by doubleness.

IPHGENEIA

Girls of Halkis, I am ready,
Lead me to the Grove of Artemis.

CHORUS MEMBER

No!

CHORUS MEMBER

No!

CHORUS MEMBER

No!

CHORUS MEMBER

I cannot bear to listen.

CHORUS MEMBER

I cannot bear to look.

CHORUS

You must. We must. One and all.

KLYTAIMNESTRA
O child, you're leaving me!

IPHGENEIA
Never to come back.

KLYTAIMNESTRA
Don't leave your mother like this.

IPHGENEIA
I wish that I could stay awhile, but can't.

KLYTAIMNESTRA
O stay, stay, don't leave me.

IPHGENEIA
I will not allow
One tear fall on my behalf.
So let us sing the hymn of sacrifice
To Zeuschild, Artemis,
So my fate be fortunate for Greece.
Let us make ready holy reeds
And kindle cleansing fires,
Lead me to the altar.
I now bring salvation
And victory, victory, victory to Greece.

The Exodus – Hymn to Artemis

Iphgeneia dances with the Chorus.
The Chorus join with her slowly and disparately.

IPHGENEIA (*sings*)
Give me garlands for my head,
Plait my hair with flowers,
Death must be my marriage bed
But by my death, revenge is ours.

Dance around the Danaan ships,
Dance in sacrificial bliss.
With my lifeblood wet your lips,
Bow to the will of Artemis.

CHORUS

The tears we have we shed them now,
For Artemis does not allow
A sacrifice to spoil with tears
And sentimental human fears.

ALL

Dance around the Danaan ships,
Dance in sacrificial bliss.
With my lifeblood wet your lips,
Bow to the will of Artemis.

IPHGENEIA

O Mycenae, O my happy home
To your halls I'll no more come.
Young girls who cry now for my fate
You must support me, celebrate.

ALL

Dance around the Danaan ships,
Dance in sacrificial bliss.
With my lifeblood wet your lips,
Bow to the will of Artemis.

*The Chorus continue singing as they dance off
led by Iphgeneia.*

IPHGENEIA

O splendid sun, torchlight of our days,
Beacon of Zeus, I must now make my way
To darkness and eternal night
Fare you well, beloved light.

*Lights out. Lights up on Agamemnon and Klytaimnestra.
Agamemnon holds a bloody dagger in his hand.
Long silence.*

AGAMEMNON

Woman? (*Pause.*) Why do you weep?
We should be proud;
Our daughter is now one with Artemis,
Bloodbattlemaid of Greece.
She lives in the company of Gods.

Silence.

You must go back to Mycenae now;
Tend to your other children.
I have work to do.
The winds begin to rise,
I must see to the setting sail.

Silence.

Fare you well, then, Klytaimnestra Anassa,
Our future parting will be long.

Silence.

May the Gods walk with you, wife.

Turns and leaves Klytaimnestra alone on stage.

KLYTAIMNESTRA

What will my heart whisper . . . ?
. . . Dresses hanging lifegone in her empty room . . .
Agamemnon! Agamemnon Anax,
I'll be waiting.
You dare seat yourself at my table once again
And I will dish you such desserts
As you have never dreamed.
You hear me; waiting, however long
To pay you back in full. And in kind.

Return to opening scene. The Old Man is on the roof.

OLD MAN

There. That's it.
The last storyscraps of an agewrinkled fool.
And since all other storytalkers
Are longdeadburied now,
Let that be the last tragedy of all;
How we first dipped our hands
In our own children's blood.

Sardonically.

But now the war at Troy is over. We have won.
New peace is danced through all
The ruined ghetto streets

By the young girls of Halkis –
Now just aging pullets starved of cocks
Clucking in remembrance
Of dead men they never knew.
But we are free. We are at peace –

Chuckles to himself.

AGAMEMNON (*off*)

Old man! Come quick!
She comes for me with a butcher's knife!

OLD MAN

At peace –

AGAMEMNON (*off*)

Old Man! She cuts the air out of my life.

OLD MAN

At peace with all except ourselves.
When will we have blood enough?

Yawns. Looks to the distance.

Dawn's white light cracks dark night.
And it is time to sleep.

*As the Old Man settles down to sleep, Klytaimnestra
appears, walking slowly down a red carpet from the palace
with a dagger dripping with blood. Lights slowly fade
leaving a dawn sky.*

The End.

A Nick Hern Book

Iph . . . first published in Great Britain in 1999
as an original paperback by Nick Hern Books Limited,
14 Larden Road, London W3 7ST, in association with
the Lyric Theatre, Belfast

Iph . . . copyright © Colin Teevan 1999
Copyright in the introduction © Colin Teevan 1999
Front cover image: courtesy of the Lyric Theatre, Belfast

Typeset by Country Setting, Kingsdown, Kent CT14 8ES
Printed and bound in Great Britain by Athenaeum Press,
Gateshead NE11 0PZ

A CIP catalogue record for this book is available from
the British Library

ISBN 1 85459 439 7